111 ORACLE SPREADS
for Every Day

Also by
Krystal Banner

The Signs of the Times Oracle:
A 44-Card Deck & Guidebook

Absolute Affirmations:
44 Positive Affirmation Cards

Please visit:

Hay House UK: www.hayhouse.co.uk
Hay House USA: www.hayhouse.com®
Hay House Australia: www.hayhouse.com.au
Hay House India: www.hayhouse.co.in

111
ORACLE
SPREADS
for Every Day

**Enhance Your Readings,
Spark Your Intuition
& Deepen Your Connection
with Any Card Deck**

KRYSTAL BANNER

HAY HOUSE

Carlsbad, California • New York City
London • Sydney • New Delhi

Published in the United Kingdom by:
Hay House UK Ltd, The Sixth Floor, Watson House,
54 Baker Street, London W1U 7BU
Tel: +44 (0)20 3927 7290; Fax: +44 (0)20 3927 7291; www.hayhouse.co.uk

Published in the United States of America by:
Hay House Inc., PO Box 5100, Carlsbad, CA 92018-5100
Tel: (1) 760 431 7695 or (800) 654 5126
Fax: (1) 760 431 6948 or (800) 650 5115; www.hayhouse.com

Published in Australia by:
Hay House Australia Ltd, 18/36 Ralph St, Alexandria NSW 2015
Tel: (61) 2 9669 4299; Fax: (61) 2 9669 4144; www.hayhouse.com.au

Published in India by:
Hay House Publishers India, Muskaan Complex, Plot No.3, B-2,
Vasant Kunj, New Delhi 110 070
Tel: (91) 11 4176 1620; Fax: (91) 11 4176 1630; www.hayhouse.co.in

Text © Kaleidadope Inc., 2024

The moral rights of the author have been asserted.

Cover and Interior design: Julie Davison

The information given in this book should not be treated as a substitute for professional medical advice; always consult a medical practitioner. Any use of information in this book is at the reader's discretion and risk. Neither the author nor the publisher can be held responsible for any loss, claim or damage arising out of the use, or misuse, of the suggestions made, the failure to take medical advice or for any material on third-party websites.

A catalogue record for this book is available from the British Library.

Tradepaper ISBN: 978-1-83782-133-4
E-book ISBN: 978-1-4019-7634-7

This product uses papers sourced from responsibly managed forests. For more information, see www.hayhouse.co.uk.

Printed and bound by CPI (UK) Ltd, Croydon CR0 4YY

MIX
Paper | Supporting
responsible forestry
FSC
www.fsc.org   FSC® C171272

" Let yourself be silently drawn
by the strange pull of what you love.
It will not lead you astray"

— Rumi

CONTENTS

INTRODUCTION

When I first started using oracle decks, I had no clue where to start.

I knew oracle decks were so much more than simple cardstock and ink—that they were tools of divination, intuition, and magic—but I had no idea how to access their true power.

Once I discovered the first few spreads that spoke to me, it was like I had been handed my own personal road map to the wisdom of the Universe. These spreads allowed me to use the decks I had collected in a way that brought my readings to life and tuned me in to the messages I received in a way that made them clear and easy to follow. Not only did I have answers but I also understood more about how to ask good questions and how to dig deeper into the language of each unique deck.

Oracle spreads also gave me a way to breathe new life into decks that I hadn't worked with in a long time. I discovered new and exciting ways to use familiar cards. Each card's message was clearer and more potent when interpreted in the context and structure of a spread—the many meanings of all the cards weaving together to add layers of nuance and insight.

As my skills sharpened and I began to read more intuitively, the spreads that had built my foundation were always a resource

I could turn to if I needed specific guidance or simply a way to orient myself as I approached new types of readings with new clients, concerns, and decks.

At the beginning of my journey as a card reader, I found some oracle spreads in guidebooks and some online, but it was difficult to find a resource that compiled unique spreads of all topics and sizes in one place. These resources were so scattered or focused on one specific deck that I realized if I wanted more spreads, I would need to start creating my own.

That is when this guidebook began to take shape.

As an author and an artist, I wanted to create a collection that was not only fun to use but also effective and enlightening. With variation and personality, these spreads reflect my real-life experiences. My own personal inquiries and my intent to receive clarity from each reading by addressing the matter directly is what prompted the creation of many spreads in this book. I personally tried and tested each one.

Life is multifaceted, and in this book you will find spreads that run that gamut of the human experience. From self-care, to business, love, family, spiritual growth, and more, there is a spread for every person and every question. Experiment with the spreads and feel free to adapt when necessary. Allow the spreads to complement your spiritual practice, instead of changing it into something it's not.

I believe this book of spreads will help you refresh your oracle practice and encourage you to see your decks in a new light no matter your experience level—whether you are staring at your first deck still in its wrapper thinking, "Where do I start?" or you are a professional reader looking for a little intuition jump start.

Ultimately, this book is not simply *more* spreads, but my way of handing you that same road map to the Universe that oracle reading unfolded for me.

Let's get started!

What are oracle spreads, really?

Simply put, an oracle spread is the way you arrange the cards that you draw during an oracle card reading. Oracle spreads help the reader to gain insight, guidance, and clarity on specific questions or situations, assigning specific meaning to each card you reveal. They bring a level of structure and organization to card reading that can make the process less intimidating to approach, easier to gain insights, and simpler to digest and act upon.

To extend our metaphor, spreads can be used like a map, offering clear guidance and prompts at your fingertips that will lead you to your destination. The beauty of spreads is their versatility and ease of use. There are a variety of topics, questions, numbers of cards, and patterns that depend on the nature of the question along with the querent's personal preference.

When using spreads, it is important to remember that rather than being definitive, they are a tool to tap into your intuition and the energy surrounding you, like a dowsing rod or a pendulum. Although there are many spreads available, it is up to you to choose the right spread for your needs and to use the information received to gain clarity and make the best decision for yourself or the person you are offering a reading.

How do you choose the right spread for your reading?

Spreads bring focus and structure by zeroing in on the purpose of the reading and providing specific prompts and/or questions for each card you draw. This clarifies the intention of the reading, keeps the reading on track, and results in messages that are as straightforward as possible, even when the overarching reading is nuanced and multidimensional. When choosing a spread it is important to consider the nature of your question or situation, how many cards you feel comfortable using, and whether the spread truly addresses your inquiry. First, think about the specific area of your life you'd like to gain insight into. Different spreads are designed to address different topics and questions—for example, love and romance, self-improvement, or career. The more you use spreads the more comfortable you will become with choosing the ones that work best for your needs. This book is meant to serve as a toolbox in your practice for you to put to work as you expand in your oracle deck journey. It can even be used as inspiration to create your own customized spreads.

How do you choose the right deck for your reading?

Whether you purchased your first oracle decks because you were drawn to begin a divination practice or simply because you liked the way they looked, most people are unsure of how to start reading. Oracle cards are generally shelved alongside tarot decks, but unlike the consistent structure and tarot card descriptions, oracle decks vary in the theme and the number of cards in each deck. Also, the card artwork and meanings are completely unique. These variations may not always be completely intuitive, so choosing the right deck and spread to pair it with is key. Take your time to get to know your deck and get a feel for the kind of readings you are going to get from it. Do the cards feature deep questions about your inner child or light messages from fairies or animals?

One-Card Spreads

Sometimes all you need is a simple, focused message for guidance, and one-card spreads offer just that—a quick, direct message from the Universe, spirit, or your higher self.

DAILY FOCUS SPREAD

Use this spread daily, preferably in the morning, to stream-line your focus for the day ahead. The card you draw represents the energies that may come into play during the day. It may also offer guidance regarding how you might meet the challenges and setbacks that lie before you. Use this spread to move about the day in a more intentional way.

Card 1: The focus of the day

NORTH STAR SPREAD

The North Star spread provides a quick reorientation for your direction and purpose, which can serve as a check-in along your journey. This is a reflection of your inner compass or personal "North Star" that guides you toward your true path. This spread can be used anytime you need clarity regarding your life's journey and even during those times when you feel lost and need to ask for directions.

Card 1: Your path forward

BEST APPROACH SPREAD

Turn to this spread when you are trying to determine the most effective way to approach a situation or challenge. When facing uncertainty about the best way to move forward, this spread can help affirm and/or narrow down the next steps. This can be used anytime you need straightforward clarity or confirmation.

Card 1: How to handle or approach the situation/person/ challenge

EMPOWERMENT SPREAD

Sometimes you need to be reminded of your strengths, and this quick spread allows you to do so. Use this spread to acknowledge and celebrate one of your greatest strengths at the moment, and reflect on the energy that is empowering you.

Card 1: Your greatest strength at the present moment

GRATITUDE ATTITUDE SPREAD

Use this spread as a tool to embody an attitude of gratitude by bringing attention to the things you are thankful for in your life. The card reflects one thing that you're grateful for to assist you with cultivating a positive mindset. Think about how you can use this energy to shift your perspective and manifest many more opportunities to express gratitude.

Card 1: Something to be grateful for

GOAL SETTER SPREAD

Ready, set, goal! When in pursuit of your goals and dreams, this spread can help you identify anything that may hinder your progress. Use this card's energy to help keep your life in alignment with your goals and move toward them.

Card 1: Potential obstacle in pursuit of your goal

ENERGY CHECK-IN SPREAD

Check in with your energy and emotions with this spread. Draw one card to represent your current energy or emotional state. Use this card for confirmation and/or to identify areas of self-care or emotional support.

Card 1: Your current emotional state

CHAPTER 2

Two-Card Spreads

Two-card spreads can offer valuable insights and guidance as they reflect the duality of the world we live in. They provide a concise and focused way to address a variety of matters, while providing twice the insight of one-card spreads.

YIN-YANG SPREAD

Maintaining balance can be difficult when faced with the demands of life. It can become even more challenging when experiencing an imbalance to figure out how to address it. Whether you're feeling out of sync or as if something is throwing you off your routine, this spread can help you achieve greater balance in any area of your life.

Card 1: What area of your life is out of balance?

Card 2: What will help restore balance and harmony?

GROWTH & EXPANSION SPREAD

We all have the potential for growth, but there are periods in life that feel stagnant. Despite the desire for action and forward movement, it is not clear how to begin. This spread provides insight into what could be causing this and why, along with how to proceed.

Card 1: What is causing you to feel stuck or stagnant?

Card 2: What action can help move things forward?

YOU & THEM SPREAD

This spread is a direct way to explore the dynamic between you and another person, whether it's a family member, friend, love interest, or co-worker. Use it to obtain a deeper understanding of your own feelings as well as the interaction with the other person.

Card 1: How your energy is interacting with *them*

Card 2: How their energy is interacting with *you*

SPIRIT OF DISCERNMENT SPREAD

Practicing discernment is key, and this spread will help you gain insight into what is serving you and what is not. Check in with yourself periodically using this spread to take inventory of the things you should either keep or let go.

Card 1: Something to keep

Card 2: Something to let go of

LIGHT & SHADOW SPREAD

This spread represents the duality of light and shadow elements found in each person and situation in your life. Just as there is no darkness without the dawn, there is no painful experience without a lesson. Use this spread to take a step back and recognize the interplay of light and shadow in your inquiry.

Card 1: The Light: What is positive, inspiring, or visible

Card 2: The Shadow: What is negative, challenging, or hidden

TWO-CARD CROSS SPREAD

The Two-Card Cross spread is an abbreviated, yet effective, version of the popular Celtic Cross spread, which generally includes 10 cards that offer advice on many wide-ranging topics. Understand the challenges and determine a solution by posing two key messages.

Card 1: The situation at hand/heart of the matter

Card 2: The challenge/what is impacting the situation

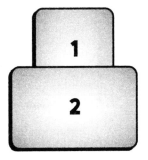

THE STUDENT & THE TEACHER SPREAD

In life we are both students and teachers, constantly learning from others and sharing our own knowledge. Allow this spread to shed some light on what there is to learn as a student and how you can use this to teach others.

Card 1: What can you learn from your current situation?

Card 2: How can you use this knowledge to teach others and move forward?

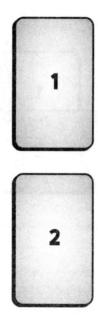

DECISIONS, DECISIONS SPREAD

When faced with a difficult decision, it can be challenging to know which choice to make. This spread provides clear guidance when you're struggling with two options by looking into the potential outcome of each decision.

Card 1: Outcome of option 1

Card 2: Outcome of option 2

SELF-AWARENESS SPREAD

Self-awareness is a tool for personal growth and transformation. By identifying your limiting patterns and beliefs, you can begin to recognize your innate power over them and take the steps to overcome anything hindering you from reaching your greatest potential.

Card 1: A limiting belief or pattern

Card 2: Something you possess that can help you overcome that pattern

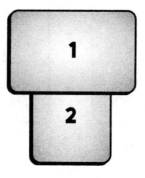

LOVE & APPRECIATION SPREAD

Shaped like a simple heart, this spread is designed to help you pause and focus on the love and appreciation you have for yourself. Use this as an opportunity to bring greater awareness and intentionality to your relationship with yourself by laying out this spread whenever you need some self-care.

Card 1: A quality to love and embrace about yourself

Card 2: How to appreciate and be thankful for that quality

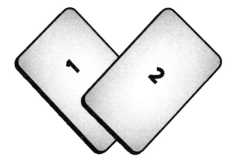

CHAPTER 3

Three-Card Spreads

Three-card spreads are probably the most
popular and versatile way to approach
many different situations and questions.
These spreads extend the scope of a
two-card spread to help the reader gain
a more well-rounded, direct path forward.

TIME TRAVELER SPREAD

It is often said that in order to know your future, you must know and understand your past. This spread transports you both backward and forward in time so you can observe the past energies that have led to the challenges and opportunities in your present moment, as well as potential outcomes in the future.

Card 1: Past energies

Card 2: Present moment

Card 3: Future outcomes

MIND, BODY, & SOUL SPREAD

This three-card spread speaks to the fundamental aspects and a deeper understanding of your being: your mind, body, and soul. Each card represents a different dimension of yourself, providing insight into these aspects individually and taken together. Use this spread to simply check in on three aspects of your innermost self, or as a way to find harmony and balance at times when the three are out of sync.

Card 1: Mind: Mental state and thought patterns

Card 2: Body: Physical health and well-being

Card 3: Soul: Higher self and spiritual growth

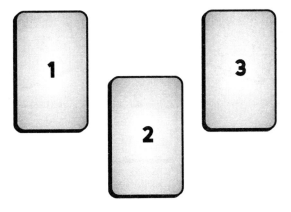

THREE WISHES SPREAD

If a genie appeared to grant you three wishes based on your innermost dreams and deepest desires, what would you wish for? Children often ask one another this, but the magic of wishes is connected to manifestation and a very real way to set intentions. So, what do you wish for?

Card 1: Wish 1

Card 2: Wish 2

Card 3: Wish 3

CREATIVE SPARK SPREAD

Divination allows you to tap into the creative spark of inspiration within you. Whether you're a writer, artist, musician, dancer, etc., this spread can help you to not only intuitively tap into your inner creativity and ignite new ideas but also find ways to sustain that first burst of flame and grow it into a bonfire that warms and lights up the lives of everyone circled around it.

Card 1: Spark of creativity

Card 2: Fuel for the flame

Card 3: Effort that will sustain the fire

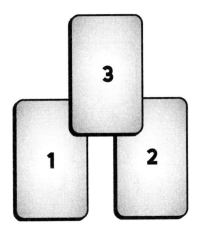

OPPORTUNITY AWAITS SPREAD

Opportunities can come in many forms, from job offers, invitations, financial gifts, or investments, to newly discovered passions and desires or spiritual growth. But change is never simple or easy, so each shiny, new opportunity will likely come with a sacrifice. For example, a new job might necessitate moving away from a town you love, or accepting a gift will come with strings attached. Use this spread to help you evaluate your opportunities with eyes open to the impact of your decisions.

Card 1: Opportunity

Card 2: Sacrifice

Card 3: Reward

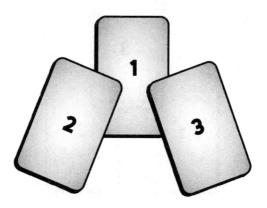

SEEKING PARTNERSHIP SPREAD

This spread will help you navigate partnerships of any category, including business, friendship, or romantic, but with a focus on *you*, not just this new person. Use this spread to gain more insight into what you're truly looking for along with an understanding of what you have to offer and how this partnership will serve you in return. Are you getting back what you are putting in?

Card 1: What are you seeking in this partnership?

Card 2: What are you bringing to this potential partnership?

Card 3: How will this partnership serve you in reaching your goals?

SOUL MANIFESTER SPREAD

The infinite power of manifestation is available for you to tap into. You can create the reality you desire by aligning your thoughts, feelings, and actions with your goals. But what if you are not sure what you want to manifest with this power? This spread will help you direct your soul's inherent manifestation energy with confidence and clarity.

Card 1: What does your soul want to manifest?

Card 2: What can assist with making this manifestation a reality?

Card 3: What is a sign that your manifestation is on its way to you?

TREAT THE DISEASE, NOT THE SYMPTOM SPREAD

Doctors can prescribe medication to treat symptoms, like aspirin for a headache, but their true goal is to find the underlying cause—the disease that caused the symptom to manifest. So too when you encounter a challenge in your life, it's important to get to the root of the issue, so you are fighting the disease, not just a symptom. This spread helps distinguish your immediate problem from the disease to find the best treatment.

Card 1: Symptom: the problem as you see it

Card 2: Disease: the true underlying cause

Card 3: Treatment: solution for the disease, not just the symptom

PLOT TWIST SPREAD

Twists and turns are to be expected since the story of our lives is not always as predictable as a mystery or a romance novel. This spread will help you to confidently read on—remaining centered and empowered—even when you suddenly turn a page and the chapter you were in has abruptly ended and a new one has begun.

Card 1: What is the situation?

Card 2: What is the plot twist?

Card 3: How does this change the story?

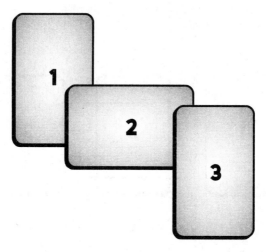

FORTUNE COOKIE SPREAD

Fortune cookies are a fun way of receiving an inspirational quote or guidance that everyone is accustomed to, no matter their level of interest in divination or intuition, which makes this spread accessible even for first-time querents. If you need an uplifting message, signs to look out for, and practical application, this is the spread for you.

Card 1: The main message

Card 2: Lucky numbers, colors, and symbols

Card 3: Most effective way to apply this to your life

CHAPTER 4

Spreads for Self-Reflection & Awareness

Reflection is a powerful tool for personal growth, allowing us to explore a world of self-discovery. By taking the time to focus on your own needs and wants, you can cultivate self-compassion and deepen your relationship with yourself. Examining your own thoughts, feelings, and behaviors in ways you had never previously considered can bring about new levels of awareness, and these spreads are designed to help you do just that.

LESSONS LEARNED SPREAD

This spread was created to help shift your perspective to view difficult experiences as lessons that can transform your life. Tough situations can be powerful teachers, offering wisdom and resilience. Discover the powerful lessons that lie within every struggle.

Card 1: What challenge am I currently struggling with?

Card 2: What lessons have I mastered in my past that can help with this challenge?

Card 3: What is the lesson at the core of this current challenge?

Card 4: What inner resources will help me overcome this struggle?

Card 5: How can I hold on to this lesson for the future?

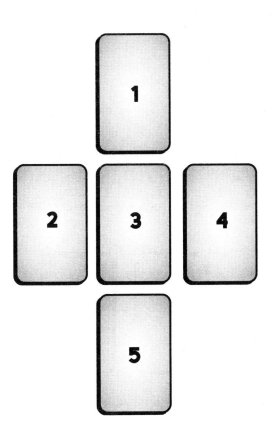

INNER WISDOM SPREAD

Your intuition is a powerful source of guidance, like a bright light on a path leading you in the right direction. By connecting with this inner knowing, you can cultivate a sense of trust within yourself and make decisions that align with your highest good.

Card 1: What is your current relationship with your intuition?

Card 2: How can you better trust and connect with your intuition?

Card 3: What message is your intuition telling you in this moment?

Card 4: How can you apply this message to your life?

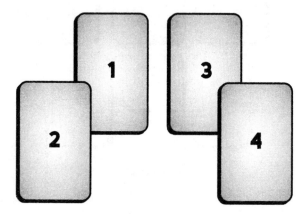

INNER CHILD SPREAD

Your inner child represents the part of you that is playful, curious, and full of wonder. Childhood experiences can cause wounds and trauma that hinder your ability to reconnect with that energy. This spread will help you connect with your inner child, understand their needs, and receive guidance to help you tap into a sense of joy and creativity.

Card 1: The energy of your inner child

Card 2: Unhealed wounds from your childhood

Card 3: Needs and desires of your inner child

Card 4: Guidance for reconnecting with your inner child

Card 5: Healing message from your inner child

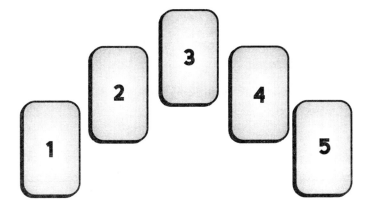

SHADOW WORK SPREAD

The Shadow Work spread is a powerful tool for confronting and working with aspects of yourself that you may have been avoiding or denying. The shadow self represents the parts of ourselves that we have repressed or rejected due to fear, shame, or trauma from our families, society, or our own brains. However, by acknowledging and working with these aspects, you can access a deeper level of self-awareness and personal growth than you can from ignoring them. This spread can help you embrace all aspects of yourself and move toward a more authentic and fulfilling life.

Card 1: An aspect of your shadow self you are struggling with

Card 2: The underlying reason for this struggle

Card 3: The potential for continued struggle and pain

Card 4: The potential for fresh growth and transformation

Card 5: How you can best acknowledge and work with your shadow self

Card 6: How to integrate both your light and shadow selves for deep healing

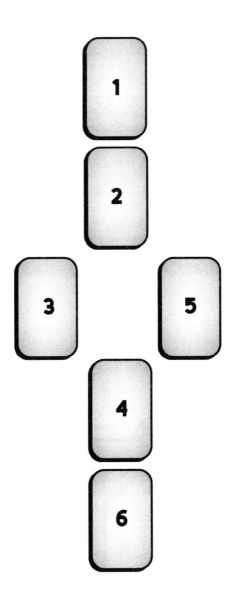

SELF-LOVE SPREAD

Self-love is a simple concept, but it's not always easy. Even if you feel it deeply one day, there will be just as many days that have you questioning your worth, your intelligence, and the very space you occupy. Use this spread to remind you of the wonderful things you have to offer and bring your attention to anything holding you back from appreciating yourself more.

Card 1: Something you love about yourself

Card 2: A challenge or moment of doubt that questions your self-love

Card 3: A positive trait you often overlook in yourself

Card 4: How to give yourself more self-love and self-care

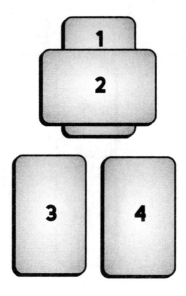

MINDFUL MOMENT SPREAD

The Mindful Moment spread encourages you to slow down and live more fully in the present moment to gain a better understanding of the many feelings and thoughts you have coursing through not just your mind and your heart, but also through your body. This spread will allow you to take a small pause and incorporate more mindfulness into your life. Use each card you draw as a focal point to bring yourself more fully into the present moment and calm your nervous system.

Card 1: Focus your body on this card without distraction or fidgeting, relaxing into the message.

Card 2: Focus your mind on this card, and absorb the message thoughtfully and with nuance.

Card 3: Focus your emotional energy on this card, and feel the message deeply.

Card 4: Focus your body, mind, and heart on this card, and use this message to set an intention to cultivate more mindfulness in your life.

CHAKRA HEALING SPREAD

Chakras are swirling energy centers that allow energy to flow throughout the body. Beginning at the base of the spine and ascending straight up through the body to the crown of your head, each point represents different aspects including physical, emotional, and spiritual well-being. This spread is designed to help you guide the energy of these chakras to help you identify and release blockages as well as receive guidance to promote energy flow and healing.

Card 1: Root | What is at the base of the situation?

Card 2: Sacral | How does this situation affect you emotionally?

Card 3: Solar Plexus | How can you tap into your personal power?

Card 4: Heart | What needs more love and compassion?

Card 5: Throat | What needs to be communicated or expressed?

Card 6: Third-Eye | What is your intuition telling you?

Card 7: Crown | How can your connection to Source assist you?

MIRROR, MIRROR SPREAD

Looking into a mirror can be like staring into the depths of your soul and an opportunity to reflect on who you are. You can be your own worst critic or your greatest friend depending on your mood and self-perception. Use this spread to seek advice from not just the cards, but from yourself.

Card 1: Observer | What are you currently feeling?

Card 2: Reflection | What is holding you back from connecting with yourself inwardly and feeling like your best self?

Card 3: Observer | What do you need to let go of in order to move forward?

Card 4: Reflection | What inner resources and strengths do you have within you to make that movement?

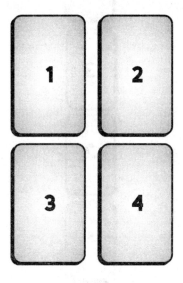

ALTER EGO SPREAD

The Alter Ego spread allows you to explore hidden aspects of your personality and understand the ways your alter ego affects your life. By examining your true self and your alter ego—whether your alter ego is simply a more confident version of yourself who comes out at parties, a childish self that appears around your parents, or someone else entirely—you can discover how they differ and how to integrate them in a positive and constructive way.

Card 1: Your true self

Card 2: Your alter ego

Card 3: How your alter ego can assist you

Card 4: How your alter ego can present challenges

Card 5: Area of your life that your alter ego best supports your true self

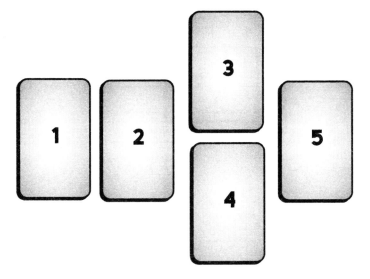

PATH TO CLARITY SPREAD

Mental clutter, distractions, and confusion can often present blockages in the path to clarity. This spread is a great tool for regaining mental clarity and identifying various distractions and concerns that may be holding you back. Use this spread to check in with yourself in moments when the clutter—both physical and work-related—is feeling overwhelming.

Card 1: Current state of mind

Card 2: Source of the distraction or confusion

Card 3: Action to take that will help bring clarity

Card 4: How to sustain this sense of clarity and purpose for the long term

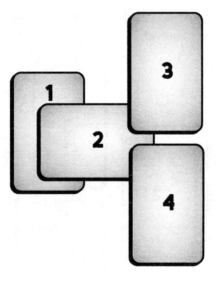

FUTURE SELF SPREAD

We often look to our past for lessons and insight, but what if we could receive guidance from the future? This spread is an opportunity to receive information from your future self so you can take action in the present to benefit you in the years ahead.

Card 1: Message from your future self

Card 2: What fears or doubts has your future self overcome?

Card 3: What has your future self achieved?

Card 4: What obstacles does your future self face as they continue to evolve into their own future self?

Card 5: What can you do now to benefit your future self?

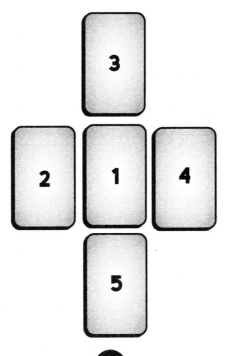

SUPERPOWERS SPREAD

Believe it or not, you have innate strengths, talents, and gifts that set you apart from others, but you may not be aware of them. This spread will help you reveal your own unique superpower and any obstacles that may be preventing you from using it to its fullest potential. Maybe you were too scared to try to save the world or you are currently letting your self-doubt keep you on the ground when you could be flying. Access your hidden superpower and think of how much more there is to discover about yourself in the future.

Card 1: Your unique superpower

Card 2: Obstacle blocking you from using your power

Card 3: How to cultivate your innate gifts to break through that block

Card 4: How to use your superpower in your day-to-day life

CHAPTER 5

Spreads for Love & Matters of the Heart

Love is one of the most complex and powerful emotions we experience as human beings. It can bring us happiness and fulfillment, but it can also leave us feeling confused, lost, or heartbroken. These spreads offer a way of gaining insight into matters of the heart, whether you're seeking guidance on a romantic relationship, a friendship, or a familial connection. In this chapter you'll find spreads designed to help you unravel the complexities of love and relationships. Whether you're single and looking for love or navigating a challenging relationship, these spreads are sure to offer you valuable insights and guidance.

RELATIONSHIP ALCHEMY SPREAD

Dive into the energy dynamics at play in a moment when you are considering entering into a relationship. By looking at the energetic state of both you and your partner as individuals and exploring the alchemy of those shared emotional states, you can gain clarity regarding your compatibility as a potential pair.

Card 1: Your current energy

Card 2: Your fears around the relationship

Card 3: Your hope for the relationship

Card 4: Your potential partner's current energy

Card 5: Their fears around the relationship

Card 6: Their hopes around the relationship

Card 7: Alchemy of your combined energy

Card 8: Alchemy of your shared fears

Card 9: Alchemy of your shared energy

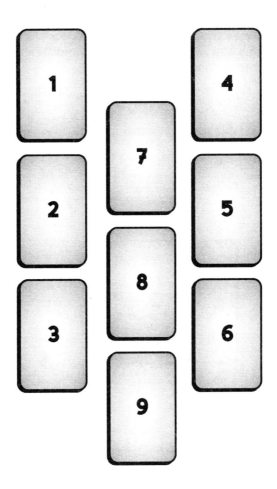

LOVE MAGNET SPREAD

Without even realizing it, your energy is both attracting and repelling different opportunities and people into and out of your life. The Love Magnet spread taps in to what you subconsciously attract and desire. This provides a deeper understanding, which will allow you to proceed with confidence or make any changes you deem necessary.

Card 1: What energy are you attracting?

Card 2: What are you attracted to subconsciously?

Card 3: What are you repelling?

Card 4: How can you attract your desires?

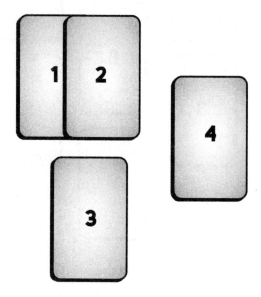

NEW BEGINNINGS SPREAD

When starting a new relationship it's natural to feel excited and possibly a little nervous. This spread provides guidance on how to honor that anxiety and make the most of this new beginning. Use it for support when you are calling in a new partner or navigating a fresh start in your love life.

Card 1: Current state of mind

Card 2: Past patterns or behaviors that may hinder you

Card 3: Foundation for a healthy relationship

Card 4: Qualities to look for in a new partner

Card 5: Advice regarding how to move forward

SOULMATE SEEKER SPREAD

One of the most common questions people ask during a card reading is along the lines of: "When will I meet my soulmate?" If you're looking for a romantic connection in your life, this spread can help navigate the path to finding your soulmate.

Card 1: How will you meet your soulmate?

Card 2: How will you recognize them?

Card 3: Qualities or characteristics of your soulmate

Card 4: Any blockages or obstacles preventing this soulmate union

Card 5: Guidance from the Universe for this pairing

TRANSITIONAL INSIGHTS SPREAD

This spread is designed as a safe space to focus on your emotions after a difficult relationship ends or you find yourself in a period of reflection. You can learn a lot from asking yourself difficult questions and giving yourself grace and space for emotional expression and healing.

Card 1: What negative emotions do you need to release or express?

Card 2: Even though the relationship ended, what positive emotions did you experience during it?

Card 3: How can you better express your emotions?

Card 4: How have you grown emotionally in this new, post-breakup time?

LOVE LANGUAGE SPREAD

We each communicate and experience love in our own unique ways, but many people believe that we can narrow down to five distinctive "love languages": acts of service, physical touch, words of affirmation, quality time, and receiving gifts. Use this spread to gain more insight into how each love language shows up in your relationship. When you pay attention to how you and your partner give and experience love, you move toward a happier and more fulfilling relationship.

Card 1: How do "acts of service" show up in your relationship?

Card 2: How does "physical touch" show up in your relationship?

Card 3: How do "words of affirmation" show up in your relationship?

Card 4: How does "quality time" show up in your relationship?

Card 5: How does "receiving gifts" show up in your relationship?

Card 6: What is your love language?

Card 7: What is your partner's love language?

Card 8: What is the best advice for finding balance and fulfillment?

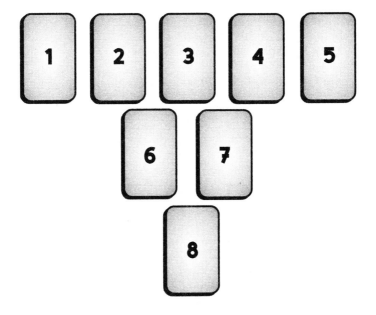

RELATIONSHIP HEALTH CHECK SPREAD

No matter how old or new your relationship is, it's important to periodically check on the health of that pairing. This spread allows you to examine different aspects of your relationship and see if some areas need to be nourished or strengthened to maintain a healthy connection.

Card 1: Your feelings

Card 2: Your partner's feelings

Card 3: Current state of communication

Card 4: Current state of trust

Card 5: Advice to keep the relationship healthy

NONLINEAR HEALING JOURNEY SPREAD

Healing is nonlinear, which is why it is natural to experience a range of emotions from sadness and frustration to anger and fear. It's also an opportunity for growth and self-discovery. Allow this spread to guide you through your healing journey—even if it's not in a straight line.

Card 1: Your current emotional state

Card 2: Past wound impacting your current relationships

Card 3: Healing salve for that wound

Card 4: Obstacles on your path to healing

Card 5: Wisdom from your scars—the healed wounds from the past

Card 6: A path not simply to heal, but to grow

CLEARING THE FOG SPREAD

If you're experiencing uncertainty or doubt in your relationship, this spread can help clear the fog curling at your feet and get to the root cause of the situation.

Card 1: Current state of the relationship

Card 2: The cause of the fog and uncertainty

Card 3: What you need to communicate

Card 4: Previously hidden or unknown factors now in the open

Card 5: What your partner needs to communicate

Card 6: How you can clear the fog and get clarity in your relationship

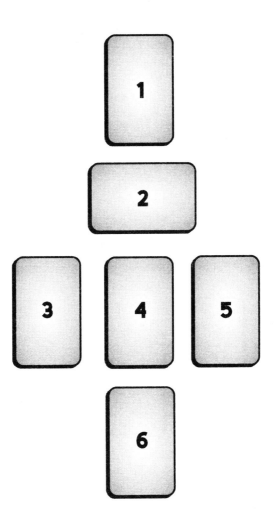

CLOSURE SPREAD

The desire for closure is normal, but not something you need to seek from someone else. This spread provides an alternative way of looking at closure by empowering you to create it for yourself.

Card 1: What was the purpose of the relationship?

Card 2: What patterns or beliefs do you need to release to move on?

Card 3: What valuable lessons are you taking away from this relationship?

Card 4: How can you find forgiveness and closure for yourself?

Card 5: What will help you move on in a healthy way?

REBUILDING SPREAD

Rebuilding your life after any major life change, especially after a relationship ends, can be a daunting task. The spread encourages you to tap into your resilience and see opportunities to rebuild your life, just as each card builds into a stack, and helps you move forward in a new way.

Card 1: What is the foundation you are building this new life atop?

Card 2: What materials and tools do you need to frame out this new life?

Card 3: What skills do you need to call upon to start this rebuild?

Card 4: What do you have to look forward to after this work?

KNOW YOUR WORTH SPREAD

Knowing your own worth is essential for attracting healthy, fulfilling relationships. This spread will help you understand your unique strengths and anything holding you back from manifesting the love life you deserve. You are worthy of love and, by putting yourself first, you can attract the kind of love that sees, nourishes, and uplifts you.

Card 1: What do you love about yourself?

Card 2: How does that quality bring you strength?

Card 3: How do you show love to yourself?

Card 4: How do you show love for others?

Card 5: What are your values?

Card 6: What are the values you seek in a partner?

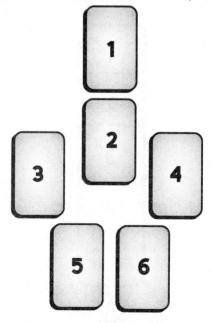

CHAPTER 6

Spreads for Business, Career, & Money

When it comes to career and business, it can be helpful to have some assistance from the Universe in navigating the complexities that come with making a living, including the financial aspects. The spreads in this chapter will help you further explore areas of your work life, no matter whether you're looking for guidance regarding your current career, pursuing your passion, or simply trying to improve your financial situation.

FINANCIAL FREEDOM SPREAD

Use this simple, no-frills spread to delve into your finances and guide you toward a path of financial freedom.

Card 1: Current financial situation

Card 2: Current financial challenges

Card 3: Actions that will improve finances

Card 4: Mindset shifts that are needed

Card 5: The result of your actions

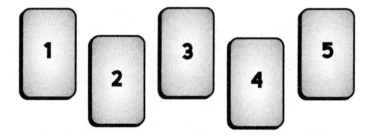

CREATIVE CAREER SPREAD

More and more people than ever are chasing their side hustles and turning their daydreams into different types of entrepreneurial, creative careers. The Creative Career spread explores your creativity and provides guidance for using your gifts to lead you to the type of career you desire.

Card 1: What is driving you creatively?

Card 2: What is holding you back from the career you want?

Card 3: What skill or gift sets you apart?

Card 4: What is your goal for this new creative career?

Card 5: What practical business skill do you still need to learn to complement your creativity and make your creative venture a success?

THE ART OF NEGOTIATION SPREAD

In business matters, the art of negotiation is a vital skill that can make or break a deal. This spread provides a streamlined approach to business negotiations to ensure your preparedness and unlock your full potential.

Card 1: What is the goal of the negotiation?

Card 2: What are your fears regarding the negotiation?

Card 3: What are your strengths going into the negotiation?

Card 4: What are your weaknesses or areas of vulnerability?

Card 5: What is the likely outcome of this negotiation?

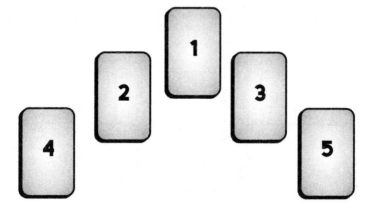

JOB INTERVIEW SPREAD

This spread is a supportive resource for anyone preparing for a job interview. A job interview can trigger a range of emotions from excitement to nervousness, so take some time to sit with this spread and prepare yourself accordingly.

Card 1: What energy should you bring to the interview?

Card 2: What type of energy should you expect at the interview?

Card 3: What questions should you ask of your interviewer?

Card 4: What can you highlight about yourself?

Card 5: How does this job align with your long-term career goals?

Card 6: What is the potential outcome?

WORKWEEK AHEAD SPREAD

Everyone may have the same 24 hours in a day and seven days in a week, but it's all about how you use the time you have. The Workweek Ahead spread provides insight and guidance on how to make the most of each day. If you do not have a standard workweek, simply use the card positions that specifically apply to you.

Card 1: Monday | What energy sets the tone of the week?

Card 2: Tuesday | What challenges should you be aware of?

Card 3: Wednesday | What opportunities will arise?

Card 4: Thursday | What can you do today to improve tomorrow?

Card 5: Friday | What's the focus to wrap up the week?

BUSINESS GROWTH SPREAD

If you're looking to expand your business and achieve new goals as a small-business owner or seasoned entrepreneur, this spread can help align your actions with your goals. You can grow not only by working on the issues you face, but also by devoting resources to the areas of most potential.

Card 1: Current state of your business

Card 2: What area of your business is stagnant and stuck?

Card 3: How can you create an opportunity from this stuck place?

Card 4: What area of your business has the most potential for growth?

Card 5: What resources—both energetic and physical—do you have to devote to that growth?

Card 6: How can you achieve your vision for your highest potential?

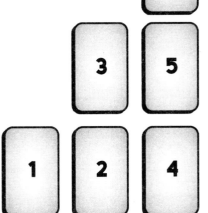

CAREER PATH SPREAD

Your career path is a professional and personal journey where it sometimes might feel like the only next step is that next title above your own or exponential growth. However, remember there is always a chance to take note of where you are, make changes, or take action whenever necessary. Your career is not something that is happening to you, but a series of choices you make.

Card 1: Where are you in your career now?

Card 2: At the beginning of your career, was your current role your goal?

Card 3: What choices brought you to this specific role?

Card 4: What are you passionate about in your career now?

Card 5: At this point in your career, how have your goals changed?

Card 6: What is your new goal?

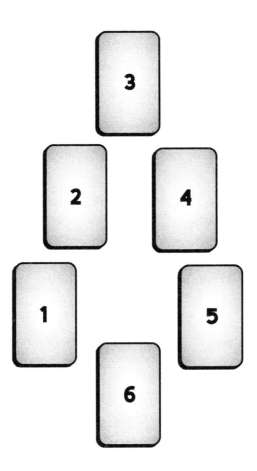

WORK-LIFE BALANCE SPREAD

The Work-Life Balance spread is perfect for anyone who feels like they're constantly juggling their personal and professional responsibilities. Use the prompts below to guide you toward more equilibrium in your life.

Card 1: What is your current work/life state?

Card 2: How is work affecting your personal life?

Card 3: How is your personal life affecting your work?

Card 4: How can you make space to practice more self-care?

Card 5: What changes can be made to improve your work/life balance?

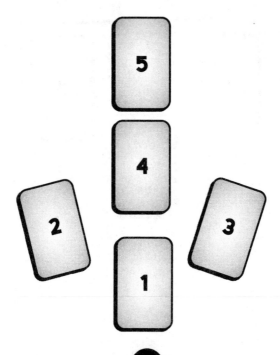

CAREER VISION BOARD SPREAD

Vision boards are used to help manifest the things you want to bring to fruition, and this spread is no different. Create a vision board with your cards and allow this spread to guide you toward your ultimate vision.

Card 1: How you desire to feel in your career

Card 2: The energy you want to bring to your work

Card 3: The legacy you want to leave

Card 4: The vacations and rest you plan to take to celebrate your accomplishments

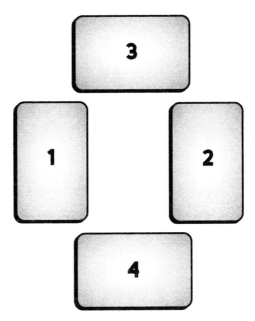

GOAL PROGRESS SPREAD

The Goal Progress spread will help you gather momentum toward your professional ambitions. Use this spread to take stock of your current state and gain clarity on how to get closer to achieving your goal.

Card 1: Your starting point

Card 2: The power behind the progress you've already made

Card 3: The energy shift that will continue your momentum

Card 4: The mindset shift needed to achieve your ultimate goal

TO STAY OR TO GO? SPREAD

The decision to leave or stay in a job can be a difficult one, and it's not always clear what the best choice is. This spread will help you navigate this important decision in your career journey.

Card 1: How you feel about your current position

Card 2: What is outside of your control

Card 3: What is in your control

Card 4: Possible outcome of leaving

Card 5: Possible outcome of staying

Card 6: Advice

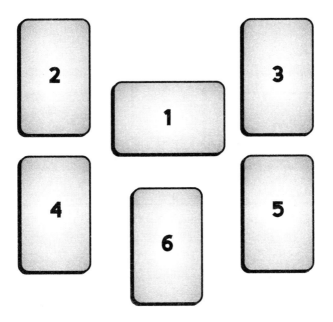

MONEY MANIFESTATION SPREAD

Ready to attract more money? This spread explores the potential and possibilities in money matters to guide you toward the prosperity you seek.

Card 1: Your beliefs around money

Card 2: How you are attracting wealth

Card 3: Potential blockages

Card 4: Financial opportunities to pay attention to

Card 5: How these opportunities will benefit you

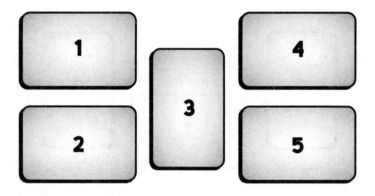

CHAPTER 7

Spreads for Life Changes & Transitions

Although they can be uncomfortable, disruptive, and lead to uncertainty, changes and transitions are a natural part of life. The only thing that never changes in this life is that it never stops changing. The spreads in this chapter will assist you with navigating major shifts, decisions, and life changes to ease your way through these transitional periods.

MOVING DAY SPREAD

Relocating from one place to another is not only a physical change to a new address, but also a deeply emotional shift from one home to another. This spread can help you feel more prepared for this change whether you are moving by choice or by circumstance, across the country or across the street.

Card 1: How do you feel about this move?

Card 2: How can you best prepare for this change?

Card 3: What circumstances led to this move?

Card 4: What will be different about your experience once you've relocated?

Card 5: How can you make the best of this move?

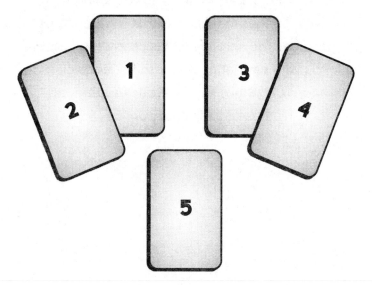

GRIEF SUPPORT SYSTEM SPREAD

Grief is an experience that we all encounter at some point in our lives. If you're grieving or supporting someone who is, this spread gives you permission to be lovingly held and supported in your grief as you process your feelings.

Card 1: Your current state

Card 2: Support from your family

Card 3: Support from your community

Card 4: Support from your inner resources

Card 5: Support from the Universe

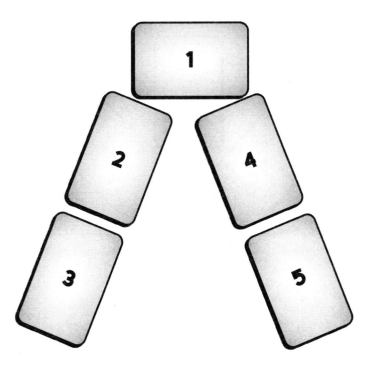

THE CROSSROADS SPREAD

Moments of major change can be overwhelming and sometimes you need clarity and direction when facing a decision. Use this spread when you are at a crossroads, deciding which way to go next.

Card 1: The root of the situation

Card 2: Decision or change you are facing

Card 3: Difficulties that may arise

Card 4: Potential benefits or opportunities

Card 5: Resources that can help you

Card 6: Best course of action

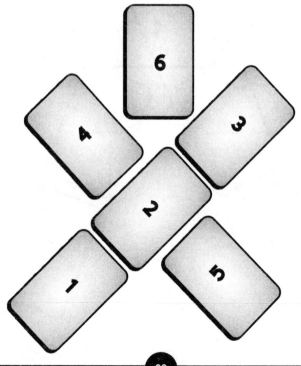

CONFLICT RESOLUTION SPREAD

Conflict is natural, but if not handled properly it can be blown out of proportion. This spread doesn't take sides and gives you an opportunity to simply see both sides of the argument and the common ground they share. Once you have that mutual understanding, you are already at a resolution, so use this spread to get there.

Card 1: The conflict

Card 2: Your position

Card 3: Their position

Card 4: Common ground

Card 5: Resolution

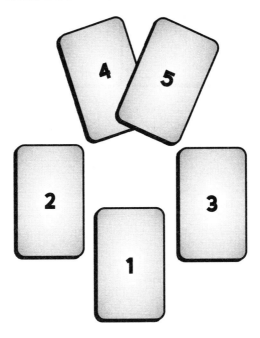

GPS SPREAD

There are times when you feel things changing or you yearn for change, but it feels like you don't even know how to pull out of the driveway, let alone start down a whole new road. This spread is your personal GPS to guide you to the new destination your soul knows is out there.

Card 1: Input the address | Where are you headed?

Card 2: Note traffic alerts | What obstacles do you face?

Card 3: Press start | In which direction should you go?

Card 4: Proceed along the route | Take guidance from the Universe.

MIDLIFE CRISIS SPREAD

A midlife crisis can be a challenging time of questioning who you are and what you want, oftentimes accompanied by the desire to do something completely different. Even if your midlife is far off in your future or long past, use this spread to find a sense of empowerment as you navigate the challenges and opportunities of your new life phase.

Card 1: What does your midlife crisis look like?

Card 2: How do you feel about this transitional point in your life?

Card 3: What changes are you being guided to make?

Card 4: How will you be empowered to take action?

Card 5: How will your life look different if you follow your intuition toward this portal of change?

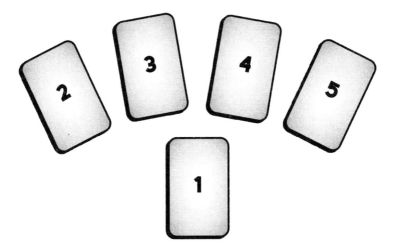

HEARTBREAK & SCARS SPREAD

Heartbreak can be one of the most painful and devastating experiences your heart must endure, and it's not strictly reserved for romantic relationships. Through this spread you can begin to process the heartbreak and use it as a chance to become strong and resilient, while remembering the strength in vulnerability.

Card 1: The source of your heartbreak

Card 2: How this heartbreak has changed you

Card 3: The thread to stitch your heart back together

Card 4: How to heal stronger than before

Card 5: How to remain openhearted with a scarred heart

PHOENIX RISING SPREAD

After experiencing difficult times and life challenges, you may not recognize how you have emerged from the ashes feeling renewed and reborn. This spread provides an opportunity to reflect on this transition and tap into the power of the phoenix to acknowledge your resilience.

Card 1: Your old self

Card 2: Your new self

Card 3: How to bridge the gap between the two

Card 4: Challenges of this transition

Card 5: Rewards awaiting you

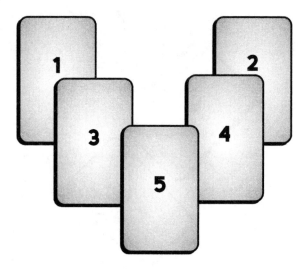

THE RELEASE SPREAD

This spread will help you release guilt, anger, resentment, toxic relationships, and anything else that is no longer serving you. As you move through various life transitions there are some things you take with you and some things you may need to leave behind, freeing your hands to reach for new opportunities and happiness. Use this spread to make space for all that good stuff.

Card 1: What needs to be released?

Card 2: What feelings are attached that have made it tough to let go?

Card 3: How will it feel to put down this burden?

Card 4: What will you gain through this process?

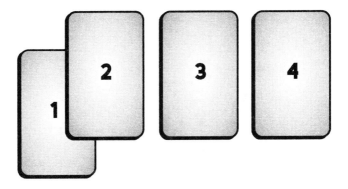

GROWTH MINDSET SPREAD

A mindset shift is usually a catalyst for changes, especially those that help you move past stagnancy to grow and thrive. Use this spread to tap into your full potential by continually returning to the mindset shift that made your initial growth possible.

Card 1: Mindset shift

Card 2: Early growth

Card 3: Old fears holding you back

Card 4: Reminder of the mindset shift

Card 5: Growth mindset potential

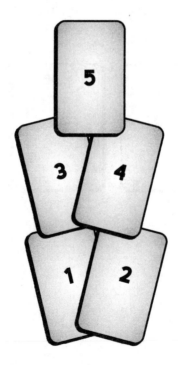

RENEWAL SPREAD

When an era of renewal is upon you, it's hard to ignore. There is so much potential in the moment between finishing a long project and stepping forward into a new one, so don't just run through that door without savoring that moment of crossing the threshold. Open yourself to the renewed sense of purpose that awaits you, but don't forget to celebrate first.

Card 1: The energy of your renewal

Card 2: Which proud moment in your past led to this change?

Card 3: What energy should you channel?

Card 4: What is an integral part of your purpose?

Card 5: What can you celebrate now?

FOUR SEASONS SPREAD

Seasons change even if you live someplace where the seasons aren't as distinguishable. This spread brings clarity and an idea of what to expect as you move through the changing seasons and approach the year ahead.

Card 1: Winter energy

Card 2: Rest lesson for this season

Card 3: Spring energy

Card 4: Rebirth lesson for this season

Card 5: Summer energy

Card 6: Growth lesson for this season

Card 7: Fall energy

Card 8: Harvest lesson for this season

Card 9: How to honor the cycles of the earth this year

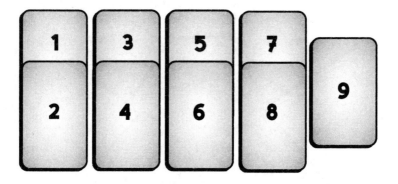

CHAPTER 8

Spreads for Home & Family Life

Home is where the heart is, and family is where the soul can feel nourished. Our home and family life plays a significant role in how secure we feel and how we show up in the world. In this chapter, you'll find spreads to help you navigate the challenges of family dynamics and better understand what *home* means to you.

SACRED SPACE SPREAD

Your home is not only a structure that provides shelter but also a place in the world where you can be unapologetically you. This spread can help you connect with the energy of your home and understand how to make it a special, sacred place for yourself and others.

Card 1: What is the energy of your home?

Card 2: How do I feel when I enter my space?

Card 3: How can I make my home more inviting?

Card 4: What is sacred about my space?

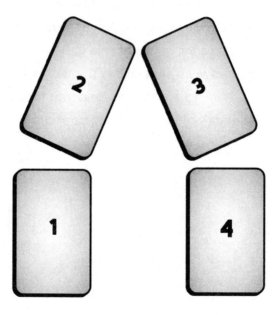

PROTECTED HOME SPREAD

This spread can help you feel more stable and secure by setting intentions around the energy you allow to enter and take up residence. Use this spread to tap into your blessings and feel more protected in the place you call home.

Card 1: What intention can you set for your home?

Card 2: What needs energetic cleansing?

Card 3: How can you protect your home?

Card 4: How can your home protect you?

Card 5: What blessings are available to you?

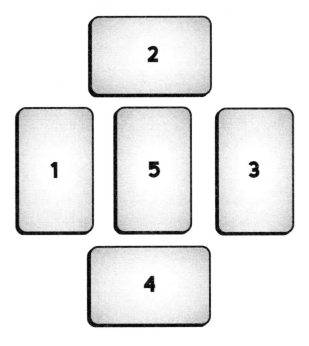

RESTORING THE PEACE SPREAD

In a family, balance is essential whether you all live together in a tiny apartment or you each live in a different time zone. Healing from deep-seated family issues doesn't happen overnight, but this card spread is an effective tool in the quest to restore peace and harmony.

Card 1: Root cause of the conflict

Card 2: Your perspective

Card 3: The opposing perspective

Card 4: What is needed for better communication

Card 5: Boundaries that need to be established

Card 6: Potential for forgiveness

Card 7: Actions that will help restore peace

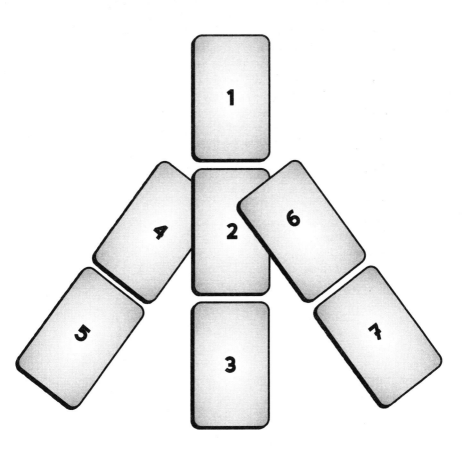

FAMILY DRAMA SPREAD

Navigating family drama can be tricky and stressful with every conflict, but with the right tools you can take a step back from the current situation and approach it in a productive way. Family situations can be complex, so use this spread to help you work toward a positive outcome in this present moment as you strive toward resolving the larger issues separately.

Card 1: What or who is causing the drama?

Card 2: What memories of past conflicts are coming up for you as a result of this current issue?

Card 3: How can you focus on this present moment to reach a positive outcome?

Card 4: What conflict can be set aside for a future conversation to center on this current issue?

Card 5: What does the ideal outcome feel and look like for you?

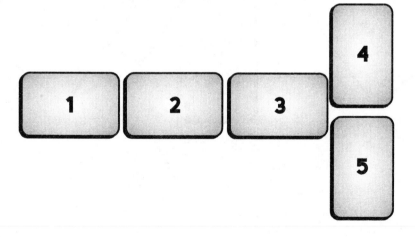

ANCESTRAL GUIDANCE SPREAD

Your ancestors are wisdom keepers for an endless well of knowledge to slake your thirst if you're open to taking a drink. Use this spread to connect with your ancestors and take in all the guidance and advice they are willing to share with you as a descendant.

Card 1: Energy of the ancestor coming through

Card 2: How you are connected to this ancestor

Card 3: What you can learn from their life

Card 4: How you can honor them

Card 5: Wisdom message from your ancestor

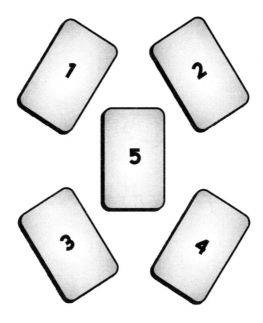

FAMILY MATTERS SPREAD

When you are a part of a family, it can be hard to see the family dynamics and connective tissue from any perspective other than your own. Use this spread to gain a better understanding of your family from the outside in and delve into how the qualities of not just individual family members, but of the entire family unit are written in your DNA.

Card 1: Your family's foundation

Card 2: Your family's collective story

Card 3: Your family strengths that stem from that story

Card 4: Your family's weaknesses that stem from that story

Card 5: Inherent potential for growth and healing

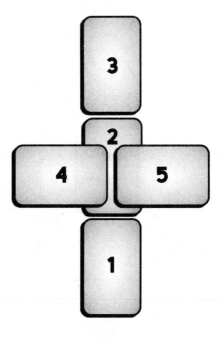

PARENT/CHILD RELATIONSHIP SPREAD

Whether you are biologically related or adopted, close or estranged, on this earthly plane or beyond, the uniquely powerful bond shared between a parent and a child has a profound impact on your well-being and sense of self. As in any relationship, however, it must not be taken for granted or left unexamined. Use this spread to check in on your relationship, placing yourself as either the parent or the child, to explore ways to increase this connection.

Card 1: The energetic bond between parent and child

Card 2: Challenges to that bond

Card 3: What the child can learn from the parent

Card 4: What the parent can learn from the child

Card 5: What can strengthen their bond

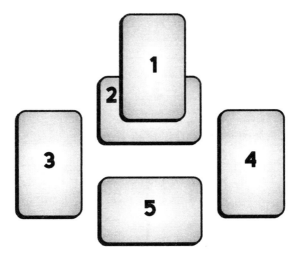

SIBLING DYNAMICS SPREAD

Siblings are often our first friends and confidants, which is why sibling dynamics play an important role in our lives even when both siblings have gray hair and instead of squabbling over the newest toy, they are picking fights and cracking jokes at the holiday table. This spread is designed to help you reflect on this relationship to provide a greater sense of understanding and sense of security in this bond.

Card 1: Your energy in the relationship

Card 2: Your sibling's energy in the relationship

Card 3: How you are bonded together

Card 4: How you can take action to improve the relationship

Card 5: How your sibling can take action to improve the relationship

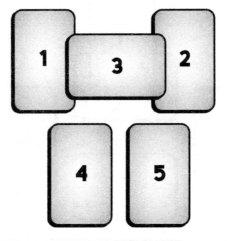

FAMILY TREE SPREAD

You are a branch of many in your family tree, and this spread allows you to trace those connections all the way down to your roots. Use this spread to deepen your connection to your family tree and honor the various ways it has impacted you.

Card 1: Family roots and legacy

Card 2: Your parents' role in your life

Card 3: Siblings or close relatives' impact on your life

Card 4: Energy of your current family unit

Card 5: How these influences help you to continue to grow

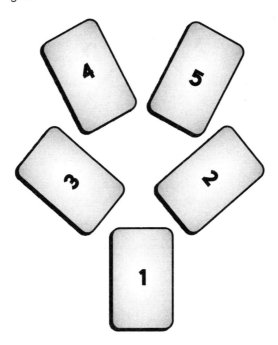

HOME RENEWAL SPREAD

If you're looking for ways to revitalize your home, use this spread to refresh and enliven your space.

Card 1: How does the energy in your home feel?

Card 2: What does your home need more of?

Card 3: How can you refresh the energy in your home?

Card 4: How will this affect the overall energy of your home?

SPEAK YOUR TRUTH SPREAD

This spread will help you to speak up and initiate difficult conversations with family members by helping you zero in on the main points you wish to share and process. Use this spread to express yourself to the people you love and who love you the most. Acknowledge your truth and give them the chance to do the same.

Card 1: What is your truth?

Card 2: What is the best way to initiate conversation?

Card 3: How can you prepare your family to listen and hear you clearly?

Card 4: Who in the group is your ally in this conversation?

Card 5: How can you maintain open communication in your family, going forward?

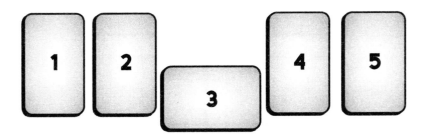

STRONG FOUNDATION SPREAD

Just as home needs a strong foundation to stand the test of time, you need a solid foundation in your family relationships and self-reliance to weather the ups and downs of life. Use this spread to inspect your emotional foundation for weaknesses and for places where you can build more strength.

Card 1: What is the state of your foundation?

Card 2: What areas are weak and cracked?

Card 3: What can you do to strengthen your foundation?

Card 4: How can you maintain a strong foundation, moving forward?

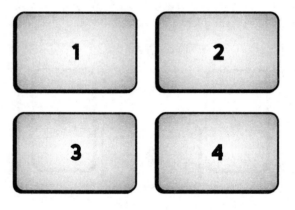

CHAPTER 9

Spreads for Spirituality & Divine Guidance

This chapter is a collection of spreads that explore spirituality, divine gifts, and guidance. Both newbies and seasoned practitioners alike can find new techniques and approaches in the following spreads that encourage tapping into the energy around you and inner guidance. Spirituality is deeply personal, and this chapter will guide you on your journey to define and discover what that looks like for you. You don't have to own every crystal and memorize your natal chart to be spiritual, but you do need a curious mind and a spirit open to the Universe.

SPIRITUAL JOURNEY SPREAD

A spiritual journey is not for the faint of heart! It may sound fun and relaxing, but when done correctly, there are moments of shadow and moments of light along the path. This spread provides insight into where you are in your journey and how to move forward.

Card 1: Where are you on your spiritual journey?

Card 2: What lesson do you need to learn to progress on that path?

Card 3: What obstacles may arise to block the way?

Card 4: How can you overcome these obstacles?

Card 5: What is the next step in your spiritual journey?

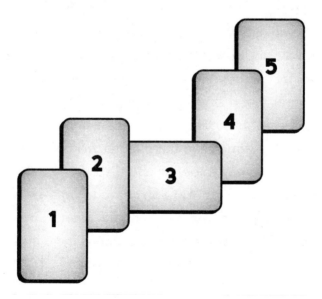

HIGHER SELF SPREAD

Your higher self is your inner guide, gently nudging and communicating with you as you move throughout the world making decisions and making progress. Use this spread to dive into this virtuous aspect of yourself, which helps keep you on track and moving toward all things for your greater good.

Card 1: Message from your higher self

Card 2: Qualities of your higher self

Card 3: How to connect with your higher self

Card 4: Ways your higher self can best serve you

SOUL PURPOSE SPREAD

One question that seems to be universal for humans at one point or another is: "What is my purpose?" The truth is that seeking our soul's purpose is a huge part of what we are here to do in this life. Use this spread for self-discovery and to gain a better understanding of what your soul desires.

Card 1: What limiting belief has kept you blocked from discovering your soul's purpose?

Card 2: What lesson have you learned from your journey toward your soul's purpose?

Card 3: What is your soul's purpose?

Card 4: How can you take steps toward fully living that purpose?

Card 5: What wisdom can you gain from your soul's purpose?

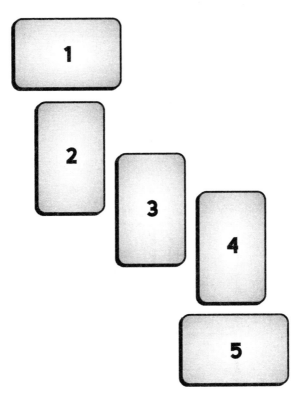

SPIRIT GUIDE COMMUNICATION SPREAD

Your spirit guides are always with you and communication with them is more accessible than you may think. Spirit guides can reveal themselves to you in many forms including animals, angels, spirits, and countless other divine beings. Use this spread to establish communication or simply touch base with your spirit guides and the messages they have to offer.

Card 1: What form has your spirit guide taken?

Card 2: What question do you have for your guide?

Card 3: What is a sign of your spirit guide's presence?

Card 4: What messages of wisdom do my spirit guides have to offer?

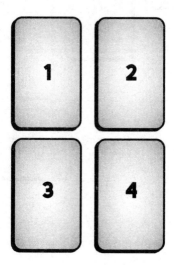

PAST LIFE INFLUENCE SPREAD

In each life your soul experiences hold a unique lesson. By exploring your past lives, you can uncover the qualities, gifts, and behaviors that have become clear patterns in your soul's journey through many lifetimes. This spread offers a unique perspective on your lives—both past and present.

Card 1: Past life lesson

Card 2: Past life spiritual gift

Card 3: Past life areas for growth

Card 4: Impact of your past life lesson on your current life

Card 5: How your past life spiritual gift shows up in your current life

Card 6: How you are being pushed to evolve in this life

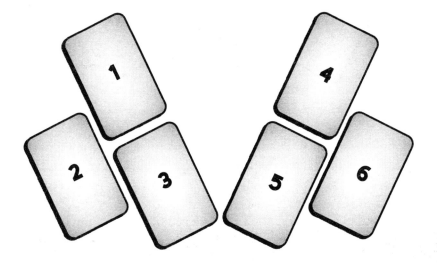

INSIGHT THROUGH INTUITION SPREAD

Your intuition is one of the strongest allies you have in any situation and can provide invaluable wisdom and guidance when you are in doubt. Use this spread to deepen your connection with your intuition and obtain a greater understanding of the insights and communication available at your fingertips.

Card 1: How does your intuition speak to you?

Card 2: Intuitive message

Card 3: How can you build trust with your intuition?

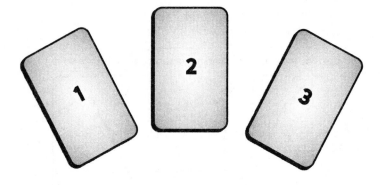

ANGELIC PRESENCE SPREAD

Your angels are always around you ready and willing to help in many different ways. This spread is designed to forge a stronger connection with your guardian angels, recognize their presence, and receive the valuable wisdom they have to offer.

Card 1: A sign of your angels' presence

Card 2: The message your angels wish to convey to you

Card 3: The area of life your angels are bringing attention to

Card 4: The blessings that are being bestowed on you

Card 5: How to actively invite your angels' presence into your life

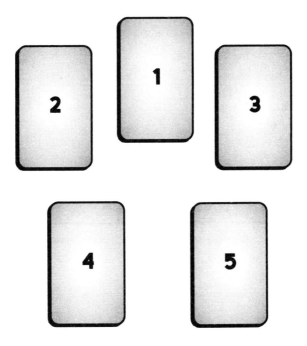

DECK INTERVIEW SPREAD

Have you ever wanted to get to know your deck on a deeper level? This unique spread is designed as a way to interview your chosen deck to gain a better understanding of its energy and how you can work together.

Card 1: What is the overall energy of this deck?

Card 2: What is its greatest strength?

Card 3: What is its main limitation?

Card 4: What does this deck have to teach you?

Card 5: What is your energetic relationship with this deck?

Card 6: How can this deck assist you on your spiritual journey?

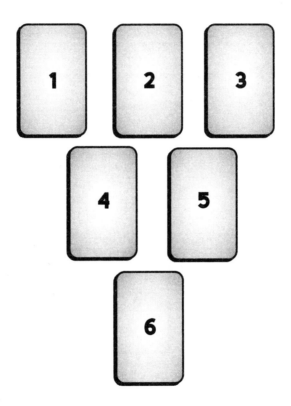

LIGHTWORKER SPREAD

A lightworker is someone who feels called to serve others by spreading love, healing, and positivity. If you are called to be a lightworker, use this spread to shine your light and make a difference in the world.

Card 1: What is your lightworker mission?

Card 2: What light do you bring to the world?

Card 3: What obstacles will arise to cast you in shadow?

Card 4: How do you express your light?

Card 5: How are you guided to use your lightworker gifts?

DIVINE GUIDANCE SPREAD

Not only does the Universe have your back but it also takes you by the hand and guides you forward in the times when you need it most. Use this spread to connect with the Universe's divine guidance in a moment of need.

Card 1: How the Universe has had your back in the past

Card 2: The challenge you are facing

Card 3: Divine guidance for the future

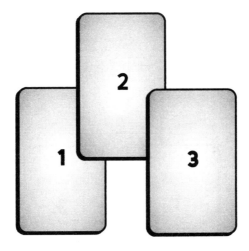

SPIRITUAL CLEARING SPREAD

By regularly clearing negative energies from your space and maintaining good spiritual hygiene through daily practice, you are continually casting a circle of protection around you. Use this spread to check in on your spiritual health and resilience.

Card 1: What is the current energetic state of the place you are cleansing?

Card 2: What energies need to be cleansed or released?

Card 3: What new daily practices will support your spiritual growth?

Card 4: How can you best maintain your spiritual hygiene?

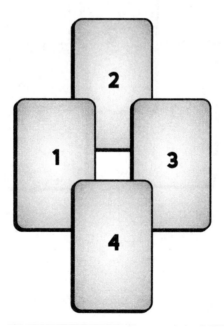

COSMIC GIFTS SPREAD

If you are curious about your spiritual gifts or you are in the process of developing new ones, this spread can help you explore your unique talents and abilities to utilize them in the most effective way.

Card 1: What spiritual gifts were you blessed with?

Card 2: How can you access and develop these gifts?

Card 3: How can you use these gifts to serve others?

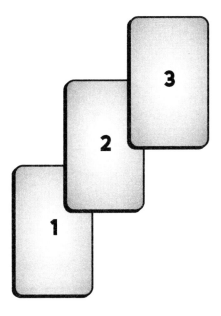

CHAPTER 10

Spreads for Astrology & Planets

Since the first humans looked up to the darkness of the night sky and saw the glittering stars above, they have been guided by the celestial bodies and shapes they observed there.

THE ELEMENTS SPREAD

The configuration of elements in your natal chart guides you toward harmony in your life. Even if you don't have a single earth sign in your chart, that doesn't mean you are destined to be without stability and comfort, but it might mean that is something you will need to work toward and seek to bring into your life. Work with these elemental energies to achieve more insight and balance. Check in with the influence the elements have on you with this spread.

Card 1: Fire: Actions

Card 2: Air: Thoughts

Card 3: Water: Emotions

Card 4: Earth: Stability

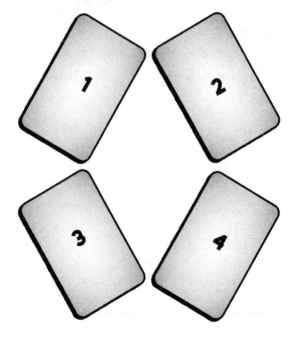

"WHAT'S YOUR SIGN?" SPREAD

Your sun sign is only one aspect of your chart, but there is a reason that when people ask, "What's your sign?" they are asking for your sun sign. The placement of the sun in the sky at the time of your birth reveals so much about who you are and what is unique about you. Use this spread to explore how your sun sign shows up in your life.

Card 1: The energy of your sun sign

Card 2: How you connect your sun sign with yourself

Card 3: How your sign influences you in relationships

Card 4: How your sign influences you in your work

Card 5: How your sun sign influences your creative expression

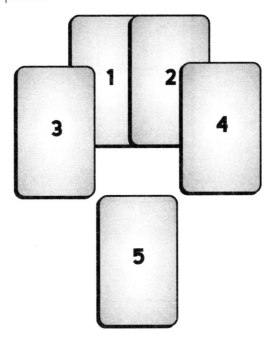

BIG THREE SPREAD

Your "Big Three" in astrology are three of the major parts of your natal chart—your sun sign, moon sign, and rising sign—aka ascendant—collectively referred to as "sun, moon, and rising." If you don't know your Big Three, there are many apps and websites where you can enter in your birth info and receive your full natal chart in just a few seconds, so go and check that out if you haven't already. This spread provides a look at how the energies are influencing you in this current moment.

Card 1: Sun | How you feel about yourself

Card 2: Moon | Your emotional state

Card 3: Rising | How others perceive you

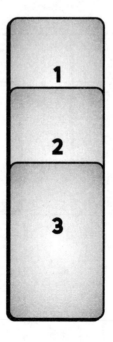

NEW MOON SPREAD

The new moon is a powerful time for setting intentions, planting seeds, and beginning new chapters. Use this spread to channel this energy to help bring your goals to life.

Card 1: What is your energy going into the new moon?

Card 2: How can you make the most of this phase?

Card 3: What is the new moon bringing in?

Card 4: How are you growing?

Card 5: What will assist you with your goals and intentions?

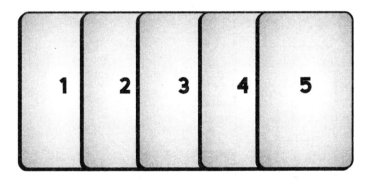

FULL MOON RELEASE SPREAD

When a luminous, full moon hangs low and bright in the sky, it exerts a powerful influence, shedding a light on the uncomfortable parts of ourselves that we might prefer to keep in shadow. This is the phase in the lunar cycle for letting go and releasing all the things, people, and emotions that no longer serve you. Use this spread to identify what you need to let go of to move forward.

Card 1: What is this full moon illuminating that needs to be released?

Card 2: What inner resources can I call upon to help me let go?

Card 3: What space will this release make room for?

Card 4: How will this new space empower me?

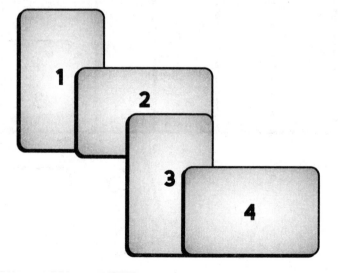

ECLIPSE SEASON SPREAD

When the sun is close enough to one of the moon's nodes for an eclipse to occur, that is when we on Earth are in an eclipse season. Eclipse season is a highly transformative time that can be intense, but being forced out of your comfort zone can lead to growth and positive change. Use this spread to work with this big change energy in a positive and productive way.

Card 1: How can you stay open to positive change going into eclipse season?

Card 2: What energies are blotted out, like the sun in the sky?

Card 3: What can you see in the darkness that you couldn't see in the light?

Card 4: What may trigger you during this time of change?

Card 5: How are you emerging from this eclipse season?

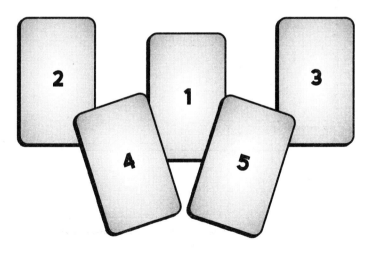

LUNAR CYCLE SPREAD

Like the four main moon phases, we move through different energies and cycles of life, from the limitless potential of the new moon to the shining wholeness of the full moon. Each of these moments contains a lesson and a natural momentum. Use this spread at the beginning of a new cycle to set your intentions and explore what energies are in store.

Card 1: New Moon | What possibilities are open to me?

Card 2: First Quarter | What am I building toward?

Card 3: Full Moon | What is my goal?

Card 4: Third Quarter | What does rest look like for me?

Card 5: What is this current cycle preparing me for?

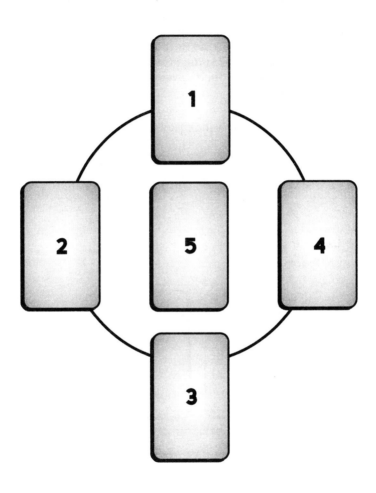

MERCURY RETROGRADE SPREAD

Mercury retrograde is often blamed for every mistake or misfortune during the time period, but it can also be a transformational time of reflection. A planet is in retrograde when it looks to us on Earth like it has doubled back and reversed its direction. This spread invites you to look at this period in a new way, opening you to the opportunities and epiphanies that are presented to you.

Card 1: What are you being called to reflect on?

Card 2: What are you learning by retracing your steps?

Card 3: What illusions and truths are being revealed?

Card 4: How will this retrograde challenge you?

Card 5: In what ways will this retrograde move you forward?

MARS MOTIVATION SPREAD

The ruler of Aries and Scorpio, Mars represents the energy of action, passion, and drive. When you tap into Mars's energy, you access a force that has the power to propel you toward your goals. But all that fire can turn your passion into anger and your drive into selfishness, so be aware of the many faces of this warlike planet.

Card 1: What are your passions, desires, and goals?

Card 2: What actions can you take to reach them?

Card 3: What weaknesses should you watch out for in yourself on this journey?

Card 4: What can you use as motivation to achieve your goals while remaining grounded?

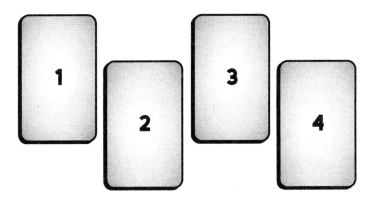

SATURN RETURN SPREAD

Every 29.5 years the planet Saturn returns to the same position in the sky that it was in at the time of your birth. Your Saturn return is a significant astrological event of intense transformation, growth, and self-discovery. Whether you are moving toward this period, experiencing it now, or you've stepped through that portal long ago and are closer your second Saturn return, this spread is designed to explore the themes and lessons from that important time.

Card 1: Main theme of your Saturn return

Card 2: Lesson of your Saturn return

Card 3: Themes or patterns you'll revisit

Card 4: How you're being pushed to change

Card 5: Your reward for mastering this period

THE 12 HOUSES SPREAD

Your natal chart is a celestial map, capturing the positions of planets at the moment of your birth. It is a unique reflection of your personality, strengths, and life path. The 12 Houses Spread incorporates each of the 12 astrological houses, which represent different areas of your life, and it is designed to help you explore these energies, take inventory of where you are, and determine where you want to be.

Card 1: First House | Self-Expression

Card 2: Second House | Finances

Card 3: Third House | Communication

Card 4: Fourth House | Foundation

Card 5: Fifth House | Pleasure

Card 6: Sixth House | Work

Card 7: Seventh House | Partnerships

Card 8: Eighth House | Transformation

Card 9: Ninth House | Travel

Card 10: Tenth House | Career

Card 11: Eleventh House | Community

Card 12: Twelfth House | Subconscious

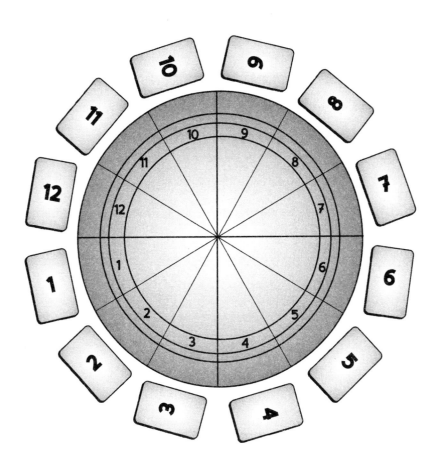

DOWN TO EARTH SPREAD

Although the human experience can be a challenging one, our souls are here to learn lessons and experience things only possible in the physical realm. This spread embraces this and dives further into these lessons and challenges to help guide you through your earthly mission.

Card 1: What keeps you grounded in this earthly plane?

Card 2: What lesson did your soul come to this life to learn?

Card 3: What challenges have you faced in pursuit of that lesson?

Card 4: How can you help others fulfill their soul's purpose?

Card 5: Advice for the next step of my soul's journey

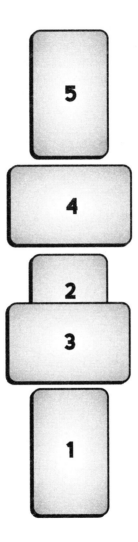

ABOUT THE AUTHOR

Krystal Banner is an experienced intuitive, artist, and creator who is passionate about making self-discovery approachable, accessible, and relatable. After spending over 10 years as an engineer and consultant, she decided to follow her passion for art and wellness. She saw an opportunity to make spirituality more inclusive and invite a broader audience to start their own path of self-discovery. In 2017, Krystal founded Kaleidadope—a creative hub that specializes in stationery, self-published decks, art, and design inspired by color and culture—which has been recognized in multiple publications. She is the author of a range of card decks and also works as a professional intuitive reader.

Visit her online at:
www.krystalbanner.com
and www.kaleidadope.com and
on Instagram:
@krystal.banner and @kaleidadope.